CONTEMPORARY NAVAJO WEAVING

Thoughts That Count

Ann Lane Hedlund

Contents

*Plateau Magazine
of the Museum
of Northern Arizona*

Thoughts

Glenmae Tsosie from St. Michaels, Arizona, weaving the first in a series of experiments for the Navajo Tribal Museum in Window Rock, 1970. Photograph by Martin Link

2

In northern Arizona and New Mexico, thousands of Navajo weavers sit at their looms, creating rugs of long-lasting beauty. They say the rugs come from their minds, from their thoughts: "It takes a lot of hard thinking. It's all that I think about." These weavers share a centuries-old heritage rooted in their own Athabaskan beliefs and in tools and practices borrowed long ago from neighboring Pueblo peoples.

Over the years, they have demonstrated great diversity in their use of materials, in design expressions, and in their motivations to weave. For each person, weaving resides as much in thoughts as it does in external appearances. It is through concerted thinking as well as active production that today's weaving emerges as a creative act. Thoughts form the weaver's identities, shape their world, and guide their woven work. They are thoughts that count.

"I put a lot of thinking into it. Even at night, I think about how I'm going to weave. Thinking about how I want to make it makes my head ache——thinking about how nice the weaving will be. It's the same as when a man is building a house and he gets very tired, or a man might be working very hard on the railroad. Weaving's like doing the same kind of hard work."

ASON YELLOWHAIR 1988

Modern rug by Glenmae Tsosie, 1970. From MNA collections, photograph by Gene Balzer

Being a Navajo Weaver

Mae Whitehorse herding sheep with her daughter, Leona, on Hoskinini Mesa, 1979. Photograph by Jerry Jacka

Judging from population figures, surveys of weavers, and queries at trading posts, perhaps one out of every six adult Navajo women knows how to weave. This means there may be as many as 28,000 weavers today in northern Arizona and New Mexico.

Weavers today range from teenagers to elderly grandmothers, with the majority in their fifties and sixties. Many learned to weave as young girls by assisting their mothers and grandmothers. Increasingly, women in their twenties have discovered weaving, learning from relatives,

"My grandmother and my great grandmother were weavers too. I never saw their rugs...but they were weavers. I was just thinking about it—since my grandmother and my great grandmother were weavers, why not me too? Now I support my family with it. I want my daughter and my daughters-in-law to weave, and my little grandkids too."

IRENE CLARK 1991

friends, and schools. Following traditional roles, most Navajo weavers are women, but at least several dozen men and boys are breaking from the past and learning to weave. Because weaving brings income and represents a creative outlet, their numbers are growing.

Weavers come from all over the Navajo Nation, from surrounding areas, and from any place where Navajo people now live—including New York, Los Angeles, and Phoenix. A few reservation communities, such as Ganado and Two Grey Hills, are known for weaving, sometimes because one or more families made exceptional rugs there and sometimes because an active local trading post drew weavers to it. Today, weavers on the reservation may travel long distances from their homes to make a desirable sale at a gallery or museum shop. Urban weavers often return to their families and to the reservation for supplies, technical advice, and inspiration.

Navajo weavers balance the traditional and the modern in dynamic and active ways. Elements of both are found side by side—installing solar panels on a log hogan so they can work at night, herding sheep on a bright red motorcycle, and attending college while making old-style saddle blankets.

Some weavers lead conservative, rural lives still based on the sheep economy. Many speak no English, only their complex, tonal language. Extended families may live close together or in compounds and rely heavily on each other.

Increasingly, however, the family unit is smaller—sometimes breaking away completely from the home community to live in modern subdivisions. Weavers now send their children to college and encourage them to pursue professional careers; they may also attend college themselves, using their weaving to pay for their education. Most often, however, a variety of ties continues to link these families with their kin and with their native values.

Religions—traditional Navajo beliefs and ritual, the Native American Church, Christian denominations, and even the Baha'i faith—play important roles in many weavers' lives. For some people, traditional beliefs shape the process of weaving: "The rug has songs and prayers too. It's got some good songs in it. So you don't mess around with a rug; it's very sacred. I should learn how to sing [the weaving songs] but I haven't yet. When you finish your rug, you always say a prayer that will help you again. I do that."

Certain precautions—not weaving while pregnant and not passing items through the loom's frame—control when and how to weave. One weaver considers that "attending the Native American Church really has helped me a lot" in more focused thoughts and the ability to concentrate. For others, Christian and secular influences now make it possible to weave images considered by some to be sacred and taboo, like the *ye'ii bicheii* and sandpainting rugs. Tapes of gospel choirs, peyote songs, native music, powwow drumming, and country western ballads all accompany weavers while they work at their looms.

Many weavers depend upon their rugs for their livelihood: A young woman comments, "If I didn't know how to weave, how would I be supporting my kids? I sell a rug every month because I have to pay my bills." For those who lead relatively traditional lives on the reservation, weaving provides income while allowing women to stay home with their families and to raise livestock, farm, and maintain other rural activities. In addition to paying the grocery bills, money from rug sales occasionally is used to build a home, buy a pick-up, or pay for "extras."

For these rewards, weavers put in long hours and great effort. Unfortunately, like many artisans, weavers do not always earn enough to support their families. Often, households rely on family members contributing from a variety of sources—herding, farming, weaving, jewelry-making, cash-paying jobs, and government paychecks.

Remembering the Roots

6

Moki stripe revival rug by Sadie Curtis and Alice Belone, 1993. First Prize, Blanket Revival Category, 1993 Navajo Show. The alternating blue and black stripes are called "Moki" stripes after an archaic name for the Hopi Indians, even though Hopis rarely wove or wore such patterned blankets.
From MNA collections, photograph by Gene Balzer

"The trader wanted me to make all these old designs and now I'm used to it. I enjoy making old style rugs. My weavings of old patterns have gone all over the world— New York, Japan, Hawaii."

MARY LEE BEGAY 1991

The development of Navajo weaving over three and a half centuries suggests that weavers have always paid close attention to the process of their craft. Their most splendid products, often traded to other Indian tribes in the earliest days, reflect tremendous energy and time spent at the loom.

The Navajos' ancestors migrated from their Athabaskan homelands in the North sometime between the twelfth and fifteenth centuries (there is much dispute among archaeologists on precisely when). Thus, the Navajo people are relative newcomers to the American Southwest, where Hopi, Zuni, and Rio Grande Pueblo people have been living in villages for many centuries. Based on significant events in Navajo history that shaped the evolution of Navajo weaving, four major periods can be defined: Classic, Transition, Rug, and Recent.

CLASSIC PERIOD

In the Classic Period (1650–1865), the Navajo people established a self-reliant and independent way of life in the Southwest. Families lives in dispersed settlements across northern Arizona, northern New Mexico, and southern Utah. During the earliest part of this period, they supported themselves by hunting game and gathering wild plants, with sheep herding and small-scale farming added later. Kin and clan networks formed the basis for social relations. Older Athabaskan and Pueblo beliefs blended to form the rich assembly of origin stories and curing rituals that make up Navajo religion today.

Olive Hubbard, Kinlichee, Arizona, 1981, weaving a variation on the Ganado Red style. Photograph by Ann Lane Hedlund

Hopi medicine man Little Sam (Pemahyne) poses at the Grand Canyon, 1929, wearing an early 20th century revival of a Navajo chief's blanket. Photograph from MNA Photo Archives

Navajo textiles soon became an important component of the regional trade system. As time went on, Navajo weaving evolved. Plain stripes were elaborated with bold patterns of stepped triangles, blocks, and other geometric elements. Weavers incorporated motifs from their own basketry, varied earlier Pueblo prototypes, and created new kinds of textiles as needs changed. The "chief" blankets and intricately patterned sarapes of the Classic period were unique to the Navajos, with no exact counterparts elsewhere. Such blankets still provide designs for modern rugs.

Classic period textiles vary greatly in refinement, ranging from thickly spun and coarsely woven utility blankets to extremely fine, even-textured shoulder (or "wearing") blankets with fancy patterning. The weaving also shows many individual idiosyncrasies—signs of the weavers' hands and humor. Although we know little about individual weavers of this period, probably most were women who worked at home, just as many do today.

TRANSITION PERIOD

During the Transition period (1865–1895), Navajo life shifted dramatically from basic independence to constant clashes with and domination by the United States government. Beginning in 1863, many Navajos were forced to live at Bosque Redondo in New Mexico to prevent their interference with Anglo-American westward expansion. Their release in 1868 brought further changes to their culture. American settlers and the military moved onto their lands. The railroad crossed the Southwest in the early 1880s. Trading posts and Christian missions sprang up throughout the area. Travel and communication became easier. Wage labor and the availability of commercial goods led to the development of a cash economy. The government boarding school system put unrelated children together and enforced new customs and values.

Navajos joined the consumer economy and explored entirely new resources. Weavers used manufactured yarns and new dyes to develop styles such as the multicolored Germantown "eye dazzler." They also

During this period, Navajos perfected weaving techniques that are still used today. They adopted loom weaving in the mid-1600s from their Pueblo neighbors, who were farmers with a long heritage of cotton growing and weaving. Navajo women most likely learned from weavers at Zuni Pueblo or from one of the western Rio Grande pueblos such as Jemez. Sheep were introduced to the Southwest by the Spanish beginning in 1698. Home-grown and home-processed materials, a limited range of colors, and simple banded and terraced designs adorn the early blankets of this period. Spanish chronicles indicate that Navajo wool and cotton blanket weaving was well established by the early 1700s.

8

Late Classic chief blanket, third phase, circa 1865–1875. From MNA collections, photograph by Gene Balzer

Transitional Germantown yarn "eye dazzler," circa 1880–1910. From MNA collections, photograph by Gene Balzer

Storm pattern rug by Helen Hudgins, Shonto, circa 1950. First Prize, Western Category, 1950 Navajo Show. From MNA collections, photograph by Gene Balzer

Modern ye'ii bicheii rug by Julia John, Lukachukai, 1978. "Talking God" leads a row of ceremonial dancers. From MNA collections, photograph by Gene Balzer

integrated design elements like serrated diamonds and vertical zigzags, borrowed from Spanish weavers in New Mexico, into their work. Although they continued to incorporate older pattern elements, Navajo weavers occasionally substituted a center field surrounded by borders for the traditional design field that stretched from edge to edge of the fabric. As the growing eastern market sought Navajo-woven home decor, weavers switched from making shoulder blankets to floor rugs. This change, too, reflects the abilities of Navajo weavers to incorporate new ideas into their products while maintaining their own processes.

RUG PERIOD

Navajo exposure to outside customs and the development of modern reservation life continued from 1895 to about 1950. Government programs to reduce livestock (intended to preserve range land) brought serious trauma to a society focused on sheepherding. Formal education and jobs became tribal priorities. Nuclear families began to gain strength over extended families as the most significant household units. Subject to the bureaucracy of the Federal Bureau of Indian Affairs and tribal government, dependent on a mixed economy with increasing wage labor, and drawn with other Americans into two world wars, Navajos made major adjustments.

Still, important elements of Navajo culture continued. Most people continued to speak the Navajo language, even as English usage grew. Native religious practices persisted. Rural lifestyles predominated across the reservation. Many communities had no utilities, most roads were still unpaved, livestock and farming played a central role in the economy, and face-to-face interactions within the many small and isolated communities were still common.

Women continued to weave in their homes and sell their rugs to local trading posts or craft stores, but weaving had become a commercial enterprise oriented almost exclusively toward outside markets. Many families came to depend upon the income from weaving. With the occasional exception of saddle blankets and traditional two-piece dresses, few handwoven textiles remained in Navajo homes. Although Navajo weaving became well known in national and international markets, weavers themselves were rarely noted by name, and their rugs were known only as works of an anonymous "Indian" or "Navajo" weaver.

The identification of specific styles by region developed during the Rug period. Often part of one large extended family or clan, weavers living in a single area created similar, recognizable techniques and styles.

Traders suggested further changes; a few even initiated their own designs. These individuals usually worked closely with weavers to enhance the market appeal of their rugs. New commercial yarns and packaged dyes, as well as a rising interest in natural plant dyes, also sparked an increase in local styles. Taking the names of communities or trading posts, early regional styles included Ganado, Klagetoh, Old Crystal, Two Grey Hills, Teec Nos Pos, Chinle, and Wide Ruins. Rugs of more general character also were woven in large numbers; one trader estimated that a quarter of the rugs woven in the 1950s belonged to no specific regional category.

Throughout the reservation, rugs varied widely in technical quality, and many observers deplored the decline in standards. Regardless, excellent weavers continued to work, and many good examples of the craft survive from this period—a time in which the seeds of today's diversity were sown.

RECENT PERIOD

Since the 1950s, Navajo self-determination has risen, while at the same time life in the Navajo Nation increasingly resembles that of the surrounding Anglo-dominated world. New housing, schools, clinics and hospitals, and private businesses have developed slowly. Civil-rights efforts, including the American Indian Movement, have increased Navajos' pride in their ethnic

ignore geographic boundaries. Through publications, craft fairs, gallery promotions, and museum exhibits, weavers have become known by name, and collectors often seek out works by specific artists.

Always a balance between tradition and innovation, Navajo weaving of the Recent period remains a home-based, predominantly female occupation. But, tourism and commerce, as well as changes in family structure, women's roles, and job opportunities, are prompting new trends. You may now see weavings that depict Jurassic Park dinosaurs or the latest Santa Fe color palette. Increasingly, weavers are approaching their work as professional artists. New materials, dyes, and designs have prompted experimentation; galleries and independent entrepreneurs are replacing trading posts as principal buyers and sellers of rugs. Sophisticated design, production, and marketing systems are moving the craft into a new era of artistic and ethnic expression.

Detail, pictorial rug by Louise Nez, 1991. Fantastic motifs from mythology and natural history proliferated during the early 1990s—from Noah's Ark to Jurassic Park. From MNA collections, photograph by Gene Balzer.

heritage and raised serious questions about their economic and political dependency. With the Native American arts and crafts boom of the 1960s, many Navajo families discovered that the arts might hold a key to financial success and personal identity.

Although recent products from the loom are still called "rugs," many are destined for display on walls. A new category, tapestries too thin and fragile for any use but decoration, is gaining popularity as well. The regional styles that developed during the Rug period continue, but individual weavers' repertoires expand and styles

Thoughts into Action

Detail, the "weaver's pathway" in a superfine Burntwater rug by Raymond Curley, 1993. First Prize, Burntwater Category, 1993 Navajo Show. Photograph by Gene Balzer

THINKING ABOUT WEAVING

In Navajo culture, thought has always counted. Certain thoughts have value that may be bought and sold. The way a person thinks holds the power to control situations and to change circumstances. For example, traditional curing ceremonies take effect in part because they focus the family's and the community's thoughts toward preventing or healing a person's illness. Thought, in this manner, equates with action and has very tangible consequences. Moreover, knowledge can be owned just as objects are possessed. When an apprentice learns songs and special knowledge, he or she pays for them: "The old people didn't put their words down on paper. They just remembered everything. Their origin stories, what they were told, all just by memory. To learn the stories, the young men and young ladies had to pay or trade for it." A patient's family "purchases" curing ceremonies the same way they would buy a western doctor's services.

Weavers repeatedly emphasize that weaving, too, takes concerted thought and hard work. Their thoughts create the designs, control the structure, and muster the willpower to sit at the loom for long hours. Even though traders and other Anglos often have served as spokespeople, the weavers themselves take active responsibility for bringing forth their woven works.

"From head to toe you are saturated with weaving. You are thinking, 'How am I going to design it?' Everything is put into weaving a rug. Then, your thinking is sold to an Anglo. Your thinking is sold by you. It seems like you are selling your mind because you put so much into the rugs."

ROSE OWENS 1988

Although not universally used, the weaver's pathway, or "spirit line" as it is sometimes called, reflects many weavers' thoughts about their work. Traditional Navajo culture encourages people to avoid intensive concentration and excessive work: "Weaving is a gift. You shouldn't do it too much." In response to this and also to their recognition of a "good story," weavers today sometimes put a thin thread of contrasting color across one corner of their rugs. Usually the same color as one of the inner panels, this line extends from the central panel of a bordered rug to its outer edge, most often in the upper right corner. Whether new or old, inspired by inner or outside sources, this break in the pattern serves as a symbolic release from the intensity that went into making the rug. Some weavers talk about their renewed ability to plan their next rug. Others mention pragmatically that it doesn't hurt to put in a spirit line on the off chance that it will add to their positive energy.

Rose Owens preparing wool for spinning, 1991. Seated on a sheep's pelt, she is rolling up the wool after it was combed with the pair of wood-and-metal carders.
Photograph by Ann Lane Hedlund

The weaver's pathway is *not* related to the often repeated but false tale that Navajo weavers intentionally work a flaw into their rugs. Despite outsiders' fascination with this story, which may have originated among certain Asian weavers, I've never been aware of any Navajo rugmaker who introduced an error on purpose. In fact, weavers strive to remove mistakes when they encounter them:

> *The hardest part of weaving is when you make a mistake or it doesn't come out straight. When you've made a mistake, when you've gone so far and you notice that you just happened to make a mistake, then you have to go over and undo it again until you finish. Then, you feel a lot better.*

The ways that weavers talk about the pathway indicate their emphasis on process, on moving beyond the product and toward the next project. Some weavers may even work an *invisible* weaver's pathway into their rugs. The line extending from rug's center to edge is not a contrasting color, but the manner in which the thread is broken forms a physical break and a symbolic outlet from the rug. Again, it is the thought, not the visible trait, that counts.

Some weavers talk about the weaving process as one of birthing. "My rugs are like my children, with individual personalities and needs," says one weaver in her thirties. Indeed, weaving is a reproductive enterprise, with attendant intensity, creativity, unpredictability. The weaver's pathway may even be considered an umbilicus whose break gives independent life to the newly emerged rug.

Weavers also talk about their work as "an addiction." The craft forms habits that pervade their lives: "Everywhere I go, I see rug designs." Some wonder what they would possibly do if they did not have weaving: "It would be boring—just sitting around the house."

While they often use metaphors in their language, weavers approach their work with pragmatic attitudes.

Not only does thought count, but counting counts too. Since ideal patterns are almost always symmetrical, having the right number of threads and using both a yardstick and handspans to measure distances between design elements becomes important. Photographs and books are valuable references. Sketches are sometimes brought out. Thought always comes around to how each individual thread should be placed in relation to the others, a painstaking and exacting process that does not always go as planned.

Humor often offsets overly serious thoughts—everything in moderation being the goal. According to most traditional weavers, it is bad form to make direct jokes about or deride any weaving in progress. But gentle humor emerges in subtle ways. Weavers enjoy the visual pun of overlapping geometric elements that appear three-dimensional. They find amusing names for certain motifs—a set of rectangles becomes a "deck of cards" with the innuendo that this weaver gambles. Other outright jokes are woven into pictorials, such as a landscape with fluffy clouds that take the shape of the weaver's initials. One scene shows a weaver weaving a rug showing a weaver weaving a rug showing—and so forth. Despite the serious toil, weavers appear to derive great pleasure from their craft.

Increasingly, weavers intentionally reveal their identities through their woven work: "I don't care if you're going to use my name, I think it's better that way. Then people know I'm [the one] weaving." Before the 1960s, an individual's name was largely ignored through the weaver's choice (because traditional Navajo culture avoids singling out the individual) and through the buyers' ignorance (rugweavers were not considered artists in their own right but, rather, nameless representatives of a primitive society). Nowadays, weavers' names and polaroid portraits are attached to rugs in most trading posts. Initials, dates, and even community names or initials ("HTP" for Hubbell Trading Post, for instance) are worked into rug borders. Through the encouragement

14

of one trader, some weavers now use "brands"—small, idiosyncratic geometric motifs such as a triple-stacked triangle or specially colored diamond—to identify their work. Weavers meet this new trend with a mixture of traditional shyness and artistic pride. A few still prefer anonymity, while others are concerned if their name is not listed properly with their rugs.

Many weavers view their careers as a continuing series of rugs. Rather than representing the end punctuation in a career, rugs are the verbs, the action!

DECIDING TO WEAVE

Most weavers remember learning by watching their mother or grandmother at the loom. Instruction is usually informal and sequential—from watching, to helping, to working at the loom, to finally putting up one's own loom. Young girls may start getting involved when they are four or five years old, but more typically they are between eight and fourteen. Experienced weavers often wait for a young person to express interest before sharing their knowledge: "It's up to my grandkids if they want to learn to weave or not," says one weaver with twenty-six grandchildren. What prompts a child to inquire may be curiosity, a model set by an older sibling or friend, or subtle parental encouragement. In a surprising number of cases, children have learned despite their relatives' outright refusal to teach them.

Adults may also set out to learn, either on their own or by seeking a tutor from their extended family and clan: "One summer when I was about thirty, one of my aunts was over here. She was weaving at the same time she was herding sheep. I think she was halfway, and she told me 'Why don't you just finish for me?' She got $60 for it; I thought that was so much in those days!" A number of noted weavers (Irene Clark and Marjorie Spencer, for instance) did not begin to learn until their children were in school. Some may actually hire an expert to share specific techniques. A few learn through local school or community programs. And learning is lifelong.

Sarah Whitehorse with a Navajo lamb at Hoskinini Mesa, 1979.
Photograph by Jerry Jacka

15

*Above: Rose Owens, Cross Canyon, Arizona, 1991. Her nearly completed rug shows
one of this weaver's versions of the Ganado Red style
Photograph by Ann Lane Hedlund*

*Left: Round Ganado Red rug by Rose Owens, 1981.
Courtesy of The Gloria F. Ross Collection
of Contemporary Navajo Weaving, Denver Art Museum.
Photograph by Lloyd Rule*

"Weaving is a way of living, making your livelihood.

Weaving is my occupation. If it weren't for my rugs,

I wouldn't be able to support my family. When I finish a rug,

what makes me happy is knowing that it will bring me

money. I look forward to buying things to

support my family."

ROSE OWENS 1991

Many weavers speak matter-of-factly about why they continue to weave. They talk about being able to stay home with children and livestock and about following in their mothers' footsteps. Many also talk about supporting their families financially. "When I finish a rug, what makes me happy is knowing that it will bring me money. I look forward to buying things to support my family." Others emphasize how weaving has opened up their world to new experiences and outside recognition: "Weaving helped me and my family in different ways. I support my family with it. And I got to know a lot of good people, too. And my rugs won ribbons, awards, money." Some individuals refer to the creative urges that weaving satisfies. And others address the importance of carrying on Navajo cultural heritage.

With so many different attitudes and motivations, contemporary weavers are easier to understand if we divide them into four general categories—professional, household, occasional, and revival weavers. This grouping reflects four different ways of thinking. It does not necessarily define the different kinds of rugs that weavers make. In fact, what it emphasizes, once again, is the process over the product. It is important to remember that such groups are only a tool for understanding. Many weavers approach their work using a combination of reasons. No two weavers are motivated in exactly the same way.

Household weavers fit their work into the recognizable roles of Navajo wife, mother, and homemaker: "It's nice to work at home because I don't need a baby-sitter." Weaving pays for household expenses and provides a certain status for the weaver: "If you're a married lady and you have kids, you will do anything to make money. Making a rug brings a lot of money. My kids are grown, but they think I will help them out, give them some money, buy a lot of food, and all that. They look up [to] me all the time."

Weaving takes a backseat to other family obligations: "I would have been finished by this time but my daughter-in-law leaves. The babies start crying and I have

to watch them." But, being a competent weaver is viewed as an essential part of being a Navajo woman: "This is my life. [Weaving] is something that was given to me by my mom. She said, 'You will always have this one, and you will remember your great-great grandmother.' That's where it came from, down the generations."

Professional weavers devote more time and energy to their work than to anything else: "It takes your whole head. You need to know science and math, especially algebra and geometry. My sister's designs are outrageous. Our mother says that she outdesigns even her. Some of these weavers are really professionals!" Intensity of work is one clue to the professional weaver. "Weaving is all I do. I get up in the morning and I start, and I weave until the afternoon." Some of these weavers work for museums and other cultural agencies: "I am so busy. I've been out of town, in California, working with a museum for three weeks. I only have a couple of weeks before my next show. I'm inundated with stuff to do." Professionals sometimes step beyond the bounds of polite, noncompetitive Navajo society: "A lot of people [in this community] are jealous. Ladies at meetings I go to don't bother with me. Not one comes to me nor does one talk to me. When I'm walking by them, they look the other way. Because I travel among the Anglos [for weaving demonstrations across the country], the others dislike me." The self-promotion of these weavers is not always comfortable, even for them, but is viewed as a necessary part of marketing. Market rationale plays into other decisions as well: "I can make more money if I make a big rug. Those ladies who make little ones don't get as much even if they can finish their rugs real fast."

On the other hand, occasional weavers pick up and put down their weaving depending on other events in their lives. Finding weaving difficult, they often drop it when other work becomes available: "I didn't have [any] work for two years so I finally decided to weave. It's hard. I'm going to get blisters on my hands. My hands hurt." Some pursue weaving in conjunction with other jobs or schooling. They view weaving as a failsafe rather than as a primary occupation.

Revival weavers, a relatively small but perhaps growing group, may have little or no economic incentives to weave. Preserving Navajo cultural heritage becomes paramount: "Weaving is really traditional. The rug has songs and prayers too." These weavers feel that "it would be a shame if the weaving got lost after all our mothers knew so much about it." Even though only a few of these weavers can afford to keep their rugs or use them as gifts, the desire exists: "I wish I could have another income. Then I would weave and instead of selling [my rugs] I would decorate my own house. That's what I want to do."

DESIGNING A RUG

Weavers talk about rug designs coming from their minds. Some say they come from dreams, others from more conscious effort. Their thought processes determine not only what the designs will look like but the entire enterprise of constructing the loom and rug—weavers say they literally will, or think, a rug into being and become mentally "saturated" with the process.

Designs, like materials, become a focus for experiments by Navajo weavers. Indeed, designs are derived from many sources and are perhaps the most changeable element in weaving. According to most weavers, few Navajo woven designs contain direct symbolic meaning or tell a story even though the processes of weaving reflects important cultural values: "The designs just get to your mind and you start out." Weavers talk about selecting visually attractive or technically challenging designs. They readily draw from a mix of sources—personal, natural, traditional, and commercial. A weaver may change rug styles many times throughout her, or his, lifetime. Thus, we can look at designs, like weaving itself, as part of a process.

Even if she works "in her family's style," a weaver knows at an early age that choosing specific motifs and putting them together are up to her. Most Navajo teachers expect each person to develop her own sense of style, even while following relatively set procedures for setting up the loom and executing the designs.

Despite an emphasis on process and individuality, certain visual traits—the elusive Navajo aesthetic—consistently suggest that a rug is Navajo. The way designs are laid out often gives clues. Broadly speaking, most weavers strive for a sense of harmony and balance in both design and color. Creating a dynamic symmetry is an important aspect of this. Repeated and reversed patterns form the bilaterally and quadrilaterally symmetrical structure of most nonpictorial rugs. Design elements fill the background space but do not crowd into it. They are spaced evenly and consistently in their scale. Border motifs echo central designs and set up an easy rhythm that allows the eye to move equally from the rug's corners to center and back. Frequently, there is a play between positive and negative spaces. Background and foreground become interchangeable. Often, a playfulness shows up with geometric illusions of three-dimensions and with designs running beyond the rug's edges.

Bold contrasts and subtle blends mark two methods of coloring. Red, grays, browns, black, and white are combined in different ways to create strong shapes. Or subtle vegetal colors and natural sheep's wool grade from one into another, offset by texture and background patterns.

Beyond a general Navajo appearance, some designs are easily recognized as the work of a single, exceptional individual—like those of Daisy Tauglechee in the 1950s and 1960s and Philomena Yazzie in the 1970s and 1980s. Some styles are shared among family members, but even so, individual rugs will differ at least slightly. Still other patterns spread community-wide and, more and more, beyond the community. Weavers do complain about others "stealing" their designs and express the ideal that all weavers should develop their own styles.

Traders, collectors, and museums have categorized twentieth-century rugs with various style names. Only

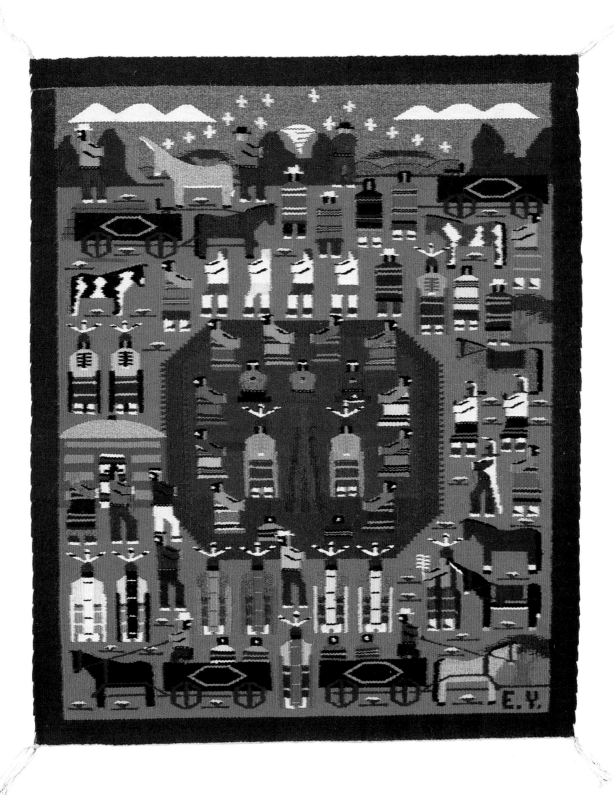

Above: Carolyn Tunney, Cedar Ridge, Arizona, 1980. Photograph by Ann Lane Hedlund

Left: Pictorial rug by Fannie Nockideneh, 1993. First Prize, Secondary Student Category, 1993 Navajo Show. Photograph by Gene Balzer

Far Left: Pictorial rug by Ellen Yazzie, 1993. First Prize, Pictorial Category, 1993 Navajo Show. Note the weaver's initials woven into one corner. She depicts a winter ceremonial dance complete with dancers and participants encircling a bonfire. Photograph by Gene Balzer

"Designs just come to you. Like, you have the yarn and you will be thinking, 'Where shall I put this color?' Then you just put it there. And then, from there, it seems like it just comes to you. If I look at pictures that I'm going to try and copy, it won't come out exactly. It might come out different. It's not going to be just the same."

IRENE JULIA NEZ 1988

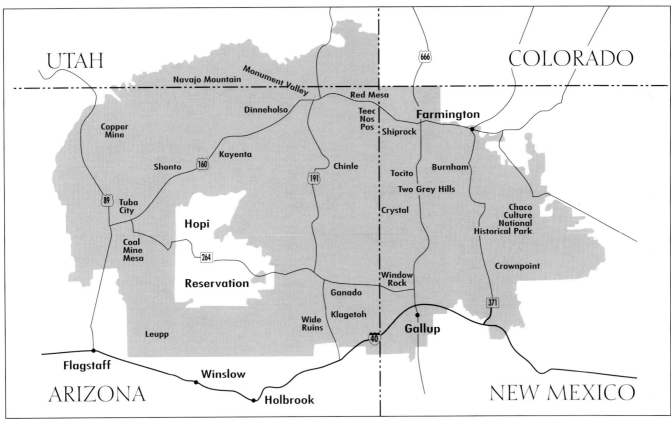

The Navajo Reservation

a few weavers, notably those who have worked at Hubbell Trading Post or museums, use these names. Some names, like Raised Outline or *Ye'ii bicheii*, describe techniques or elements of design. Most, however, relate historically to the community or trading post where the design became well known in the marketplace and reinforced in the weavers' minds—Ganado, Two Grey Hills, Wide Ruins, Crystal, and so forth. A few colorful names such as Storm Pattern and Thunder Trail evoke stories that were likely fabricated by traders and other non-Navajos, but which have worked their way into contemporary Navajo lore. Today, weavers often work within a regional tradition, but many are just as likely to borrow styles with faraway place names. While many weavers know the English names for the rugs they weave, they often are much less aware of other rug styles and style names.

While the basic elements of certain regional styles like Ganado and Wide Ruins have been consistently recognizable since the 1930s or earlier, the overall design of Navajo rugs has changed subtly. In particular, since 1960, there has been a marked increase in the number and elaboration of motifs, along with an augmentation of

the colors. A Storm Pattern rug of the 1960s and one of the 1990s, for instance, share the same basic layout, but the recent rug may have more and smaller design elements. Because of refined tools, materials, and expectations, recent weaving is also, by and large, more technically proficient. Leaving the relative simplicity of earlier periods behind, weavers of the eighties and nineties have gone for "baroque."

During the past four decades, several styles have evolved toward similar ends. The layouts of many Ganado, Klagetoh, Two Grey Hills, and Burntwater rugs have converged into a single, generalized format that includes a central diamond (or double diamond), various filler motifs, and a surrounding border. Earlier models of the four styles were distinguished by the distinct character of their elements and layout—Ganado by balanced stepped motifs and more open space; Klagetoh by more vertical and more rectilinear, comb-edged patterning; Two Grey Hills by its elements' smaller scale, denser packing and blockier, repetitive right-angle and fret motifs; Burntwater by a combination of stepped and serrate edgings and concentrically placed elements. Bill Malone of

Shonto Trading Post, 1979. Remote posts like this still serve many functions within Navajo communities—gas station, grocery and hardware store, and social center. Photograph by Jerry Jacka

Hubbell Trading Post is among those who have noted that the four now often appear essentially the same except for their colors. Malone commissioned a weaver to make a sampler rug showing four versions of the same pattern, each with a different color scheme.

New styles, or new combinations of old styles, continue to crop up from time to time. Until the late 1960s, the Burntwater style was not known. Then, several weavers from the Burntwater area combined the vegetal colors known from nearby Wide Ruins and Pine Springs with a central diamond and borders more like Two Grey Hills or Ganado patterns. A special issue of *Arizona Highways* magazine in 1974 carried illustrations of several superb Burntwater rugs, and the style's reputation was made. Such rugs became even more popular throughout the Navajo Nation during the 1980s when yarns in widely ranging vegetal colors became commercially available.

Another type, dubbed the Newlands style by Sanders area trader Bruce Burnham, grew out of the relocation of Coal Mine Mesa families to the Sanders area because of the Navajo-Hopi land dispute. Heavily dependent on rug sales, these weavers combined the Coal Mine Mesa Raised Outline technique with Teec Nos Pos and other elaborate geometric designs.

Still another style resulted from the efforts of an extended family from Burnham, New Mexico, who decided to create distinctive rugs by combining the fine, natural-colored sheep's wool from neighboring Two Grey Hills with pictorial elements from Navajo lore—baskets and pottery, *ye'ii bicheii* figures, howling coyotes, and dramatic desert landscapes. People in other communities, including La Plata, Colorado, and Blanding, Utah, have attempted to establish their own "regional" styles too.

Many rugs do not belong to a standard category. Often termed part of a "general style," these weavings account for more than forty percent of overall production. Whether they are isolated experiments or part of a weaver's regular repertoire, they represent original creative efforts that still conform to a general Navajo style.

Several other trends beyond changes in style are notable since the 1960s. The overall amount of patterning has increased, and weavers pack in as much design and as many colors as possible. Some weavers have taken to signing their rugs with either a full name, their initials, or a small "brand." The rage for tiny miniature rugs woven in the full array of Navajo rug styles has risen. And chief blanket, sarape, and Germantown patterns are enjoying a revival. Weavers often borrow these patterns from books showing nineteenth-century textiles.

From time to time, Navajo weavers have accepted commissions to create textiles for others. Orders range from modest wall hangings with fraternal society emblems and trading post logos to major artworks such as those designed by painter Kenneth Noland and woven under the direction of New Yorker Gloria F. Ross. One collector has commissioned a series of elaborate sandpainting rugs drawn directly from Navajo healing ceremonies. Weavers appear to move easily from their own designs to those from special orders; they even make them side by side. Still in control of production, they do not feel any loss of integrity in this. In fact, they often earn considerable satisfaction *and* income from these collaborations.

23

Burntwater and Wide Ruins rugs by members of the Spencer family—Marjorie Spencer and her daughters Brenda Spencer, Geneva Shabi, Irma Owens, and Vera Spencer, 1993. Their pastel color palette comes from yarns they buy at Burnham Trading Post; their designs come from their rich imaginations.
Photograph by Gene Balzer

Emma Seaton, near Paiute Mesa, 1981, seated on a Pendleton blanket.
Depending on the colors of the rug that she is weaving, the stepped diamond pattern could
be called either a Ganado, Klagetoh, Two Grey Hills, or Burntwater style.
Photograph by Jerry Jacka

MAKING A RUG

Weavers speak readily about the materials and steps necessary to make a rug. They spend long hours sitting at the loom, and the lengthy process naturally becomes a focus for discussion. After all, their choices determine the success or failure of the rug. Choosing the right weight of yarn or an appropriate shade of yellow can make a big difference.

Navajo rugs are woven on an upright loom with simple wooden hand tools. No mechanical shortcuts lessen the time-consuming and painstaking tasks of positioning each thread and packing them into a sturdy fabric. Most rugs are made with a standard tapestry weave. The weaver interlaces the horizontal weft yarns,

over-one, under-one, across the fixed, vertical warp yarns, completely covering them. She changes the weft yarn colors to create the rug's designs. In most rugs, several heavier cords are twined along all four edges to form a strong and sometimes colorful selvage, with yarn tassels at each corner.

Other techniques appear on occasion. Mohair tufting gives a shaggy pile effect. Twill weaves contain a different interlacing (usually under-two, over-two) that creates herringbone, zigzag, and diamond patterns. Two-faced weaves result in the two sides of a rug having different designs. Each technique requires special knowledge, and only a few weavers practice all of them.

The use of imported materials cuts short the time-consuming processes of carding and spinning raw wool into yarn and collecting and brewing dye plants. Late nineteenth-century practices set the stage for today's eclectic choices of raw materials. Weavers then used commercial cloth as a source for bright raveled yarns, colored their wools with packaged aniline dyes, and incorporated three- and four-ply commercial yarns into their hand-woven fabrics. Contemporary weavers have an even wider selection of materials. High-quality processed materials have been available since the early 1980s, while a narrower selection of ready-made ones has been around for over a century.

Less hand-carded and handspun wool is used in Navajo rugs and tapestries as each year goes by. Weavers buy cleaned, carded, and dyed wool ("processed wool," "tops" or "roving") from large spools or in loose hanks, ready to split and spin. They use four-ply knitting worsted "as is" or retwist it on a hand spindle to tighten and firm up the texture. They can also split it into separate strands for a very fine yarn. Single yarns (made of one strand, not plied) are bought ready to use or to be top-dyed. They can closely resemble handspun yarns. The best way to identify them in a completed rug is to compare them with the textures, colors, and weights of unwoven skeins of yarn.

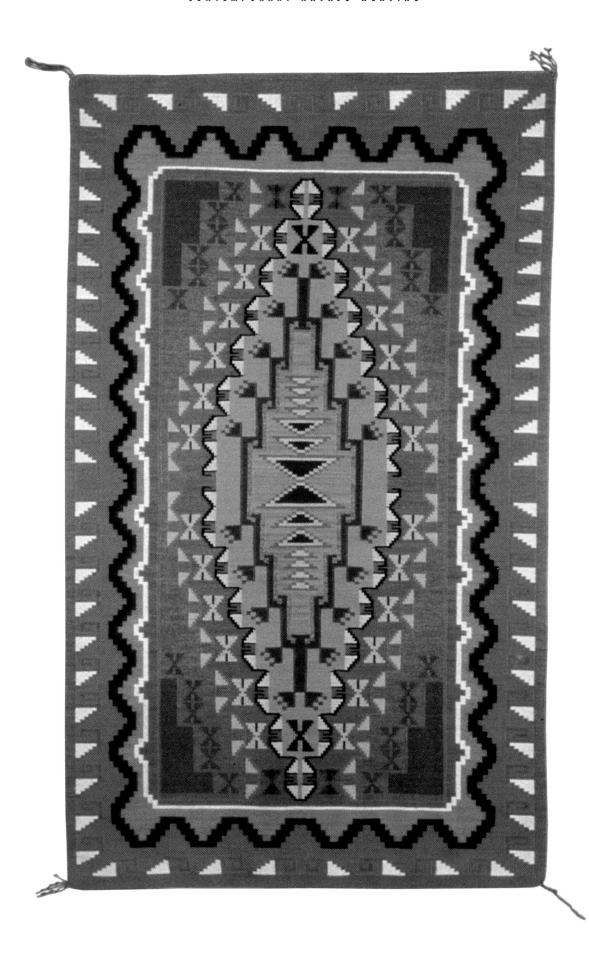

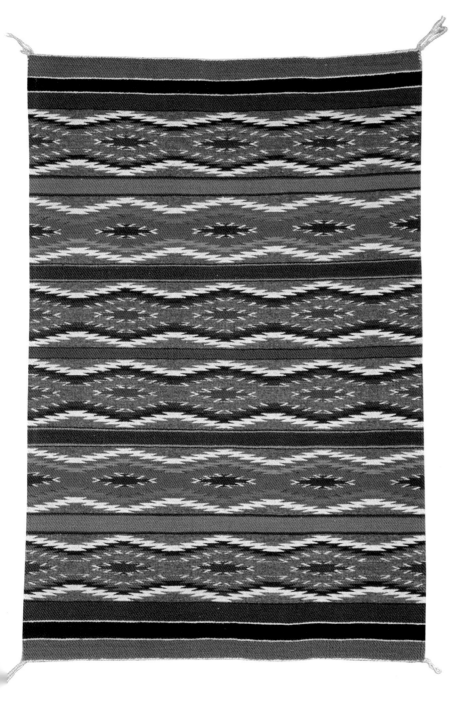

*Above: Vegetal-dyed yarns at Burnham Trading Post,
Sanders, Arizona, 1986.
Photograph by Ann Lane Hedlund*

*Left: Wide Ruins rug by Philomena Yazzie, 1972–1973.
This weaver was first in her area to move from making
banded Wide Ruins rugs, like this, to a bordered, central
diamond style in the same vegetal-dyed colors.
The new style came to be called Burntwater, with elaborate
borders and distinctive plant-dyed colors.
From MNA collections, photograph by Gene Balzer*

*Far left: Burntwater rug by Mary Sheppard, 1986.
First Prize, Burntwater Category, 1987 Navajo Show.
From MNA collections, photograph by Gene Balzer*

Wide Ruins Trading Post, 1977. Many reservation posts have been replaced by "Quik Marts" and larger shopping centers in the reservation's major growth centers and border towns. Now, weavers often sell their rugs to galleries and specialty stores throughout the Southwest. Photograph by Jerry Jacka

28

Weavers obtain their materials at trading posts and suppliers and in department stores of larger reservation and border communities. They also order them by mail from weaving specialty shops in the United States and Canada. A few traders actively seek improved yarns for rug weaving and work closely with mills, weavers, and dyers. The Navajo Wool Grower's Marketing Industry, a tribal enterprise, was established in 1971 to promote native wool production and use. Operating out of Shiprock, New Mexico, the Industry's warehouse sells both raw and processed wool to weavers. A Utah State University program to revive the old-style *churro* sheep on the Navajo reservation also has supplied weavers with fleeces and yarn.

Dyes are confusing to many collectors because of their many possible sources and combinations. Home-dyed colors made from native plants are still seen though they are increasingly rare. Competing with them are commercial yarns that are "vegetal" colored but dyed at a mill with commercial aniline (synthetic) colorants. Also, any of these dyes—plant, synthetic, or a combination—may be applied to either handspun or commercial yarns, often by Navajo women who specialize in dyeing.

One trader gives such experts large quantities of white yarn, pays them to dye it in lovely vegetal tones, and then resells the yarns by the skein or in color-blended "kits" to weavers. Even though it is hard to know precisely what was used for the dyes, the pastel colors that result are definitely appealing.

A new synthetic color palette also has emerged during the 1990s—a deep indigo-like blue and a range of bright and dark reds billed as "classic" and "transitional" colors, harking back to the nineteenth-century use of indigo, cochineal-dyed bayeta, and early orange-red anilines. Today's weavers are using ready-made yarns dyed with these colors in their modern versions of the chief blanket and other textile revivals.

Modern, ready-made materials have encouraged many weavers not to give up the craft. They also have inspired those who might not have begun. The large amounts of high-quality, processed wool and yarns now available have clearly increased production rates. While certain commercial materials—shiny nylon fibers and fluorescent dyes, for example—have perhaps lowered the aesthetic standards of some weaving, both good and bad results can be produced with either commercial or hand-processed materials. It all comes back to each individual weaver's judgment and ability to handle her selected materials.

Buying And Collecting Navajo Rugs

Because of the eclectic nature of Navajo weaving, there is something for everyone today—small rugs or large, elaborate or simple, bright or subtle, soft or scratchy. If you are buying just one rug, it will likely become a personal reminder of your experiences in or around Navajo country. For a collection, your focus might broaden to representative examples of different regional styles, a selection from a particular area or family, or unusual and idiosyncratic rugs. Some buyers choose to support younger artists—many trading posts and craft fairs record the weaver's age and attach a photograph of the weaver to her rug.

My cardinal rule for collecting is to see all you can and buy what you personally like (and, of course, can afford). Shop around and do not hesitate to unfold, unroll, hang up, and place on the floor many, many rugs until you find those you're considering for purchase. Compare the different weights and textures of the materials and weaves to see what is pleasing to your touch and appropriate for your intended use. Seek quality workmanship—make sure the rug's corners are square and don't curl excessively; that it will hang or lie flat; that the weave texture is relatively uniform, without bald spots or overly lumpy areas; and that the colors are evenly toned and not bleeding. Become familiar with the ready-made yarns and dyes available to weavers (you can see these hanging in many trading posts), and compare them to those in the finished product. Do not be discouraged by the judicious use of commercial materials in handwoven rugs because, after all, these may be the incentive the weaver needed to spend long hours at her loom (instead of in the shearing shed and with her hand spindle).

There are many posts, rug rooms, museum shops, and galleries where rugs can be purchased in the Southwest (and across the country). I suggest that buyers concentrate on reputable dealers, many of whom advertise in magazines like *American Indian Art*, are members of the Indian Arts and Crafts Association, and are affiliated with national, state, and tribal park systems or with museums. Listen for recommendations by collectors and other reliable sources. Consider that collecting, too, is a process. As one weaver comments: "If people would come out and travel across the [Navajo] Nation, then they would have a better idea of how the product is made, rather than [just] seeing a finished rug in a trading post."

In recent years, more weavers have begun to sell directly to consumers at craft fairs and through personal contacts. Increasingly, weavers accept special orders and commissions even though buying directly presents certain challenges because negotiations are often carried out without telephones and in Navajo rather than English. The rewards for both buyer and seller can be worthwhile. Most buyers, however, find reservation traders and other gallery owners helpful and informative.

Annual events like the Navajo Show at the Museum of Northern Arizona, Gallup's Inter-Tribal Ceremonial, Indian Market in Santa Fe, and other museum-sponsored fairs offer good opportunities for rug buyers. Watch also for rug auctions held every six weeks at Crownpoint, New Mexico. Other auctions have been held in Tuba City, Ganado, and other reservation communities. Be sure and arrive in time for the preview (and, at Crownpoint, a Navajo taco dinner!) so you can survey the available rugs carefully before they go "on the block." If you have already done some comparative shopping, you will have a better idea of what you are looking at.

Looking to the Future

"I use a lot of different kinds of bushes and herbs

as dyes. But the weavers are younger today.

They have more designs in their rugs. They use a lot

of different colors. I think they learn a lot from

school, you know? They're mostly educated people.

They know how to put the colors together and all

that. They blend in more colors."

PHILOMENA YAZZIE 1988

30

And the future? Younger people are certainly learning to make rugs today, and their results are often glorious to behold. But with the Navajos' emphasis on autonomy, there is no assurance that weaving will continue as it does today. As weaver Bessie Barber said, "Well, I told my daughter that it's all up to her. If she wants to work when she graduates, she can do that; but if she's more interested in weaving, well, she can do that. It all depends on what happens when she graduates."

One serious challenge to the future is the younger generation's access to in-depth traditional knowledge. English has become the primary language around the Navajo Nation. Without the native language, young people are unable to learn the older weaving stories and songs. However, reservation-wide school programs and farsighted individual families today are reinforcing the importance of the Navajo language. And the Navajos' account of weaving is continuously redefined. Cultural preservation continues while Navajo society avoids being frozen in time.

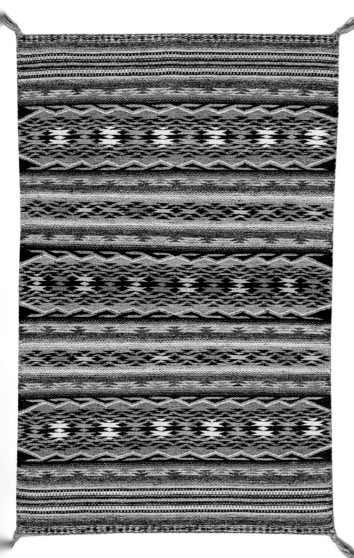

Above: Miniature rugs by Herman Brown, Lula Brown, Matilda Yazzie, and Nellie S. Yazzie, 1993. These popular items were featured in the 1993 MNA Navajo Artist Exhibition. Photograph by Gene Balzer

Left: Recent rug by Vera Spencer, 1993. In a successful experiment, this young weaver combined finely spun yarns in natural, undyed colors with a Wide Ruins banded and serrate pattern. Most often, these yarns would appear in Two Grey Hills rugs, and Wide Ruins patterns would appear in vegetal-dyed colors. Photograph by Gene Balzer

Far left: Sisters Lenah (in the orange T-shirt) and Gloria Begay, making their first rugs, 1981. Both girls have since attended college. Lenah is now raising a young son and Gloria is completing her bachelor's degree at the University of Oklahoma. One of Gloria's rugs is in The Gloria F. Ross Collection at the Denver Art Museum, along with pieces by her mother, Mary Lee Begay, and grandmother, Grace Henderson Nez. Photograph by Ann Lane Hedlund

Some of the older, collective traditions are slowly replaced with new, individualistic thoughts about weaving as contemporary art. Weavers are beginning to struggle tacitly with how to express their ethnic and personal heritage in the designs; how to convey emotions through color, texture, and form; how to contend with modern aesthetic and technical challenges. As an artist, each weaver must take responsibility for the work—both as an extension of tradition and as an evolving art form. Rugs' outward appearances may change; colors tend to follow decorator trends and patterns reflect the latest fads. But the weavers' own thoughts about flexibility and change and the value they place upon concentration and time spent creatively, these are what will carry Navajo weaving into the twenty-first century and beyond.

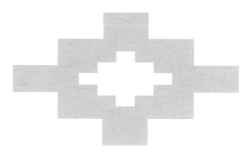

A WORD FROM THE AUTHOR

I first became acquainted with Navajo weaving when I attended Prescott College in Arizona and went out on many camping trips around Navajo country. I remember bales of raw sheep's wool stacked high on the porch of remote Inscription House Trading Post in the early 1970s. By the late 1970s, under the guidance of Dr. Joe Ben Wheat, I had examined rugs in many museum collections across the country and in southwestern trading posts and galleries. In 1979 I began visiting Navajo weavers while I was employed as guest curator at the Navajo Tribal Museum in Window Rock. My dissertation was an ethnographic study of weavers in one community—Kinlichee—in the central part of the Navajo Nation. Throughout the 1980s, gathering together and curating rugs and tapestries for the Denver Art Museum's Gloria F. Ross Collection of Contemporary Navajo Weaving, I had more opportunities to come to know weavers from all over the reservation.

I spent time with weavers and their families at home, in their sheep camps, in trading posts, and wherever they travel. Through the years, I've maintained friendships and expanded my professional relationships with many of them.

ABOUT THE AUTHOR

Ann Lane Hedlund is Associate Professor of Anthropology and Director of the Museum Studies Program at Arizona State University in Tempe. She received her Ph.D. at the University of Colorado, Boulder and is a Research Associate at the Museum of Northern Arizona.

FURTHER READING

Bennett, Noël
1971 *Working with the Wool: How to Weave a Navajo Rug.* Flagstaff, AZ: Northland Press.
1974 *The Weaver's Pathway: A Clarification of the "Spirit Trail" in Navajo Weaving.* Flagstaff, AZ: Northland Press.
1979 *Designing with the Wool: Advanced Techniques in Navajo Weaving.* Flagstaff, AZ: Northland Press.

Dedera, Don
1975 *Navajo Rugs: How to Find, Evaluate, Buy and Care for Them.* Flagstaff, AZ: Northland Press.

Dockstader, Frederick J.
1987 *The Song of the Loom: New Traditions in Navajo Weaving.* New York: Hudson Hills Press, in association with the Montclair Art Museum.

Hedlund, Ann Lane
1988 *Current Trends in Navajo Weaving. Art from the Navajo Loom,* edited by Nancy J. Blomberg *Terra* 26(5):15-20. The Natural History Museum of Los Angles County, Los Angles, CA.
1992 *Reflections of the Weaver's World: The Gloria F. Ross Collection.* Denver, CO: Denver Art Museum (distributed by University of Washington Press).

Kent, Kate Peck
1985 *Navajo Weaving: Three Centuries of Change.* Santa Fe, NM: School of American Research Press.

Wheat, Joe Ben
1981 Early Navajo Weaving. *Plateau* 52(4):2-9. Museum of Northern Arizona, Flagstaff, AZ.

ACKNOWLEDGMENTS

I am grateful to the many Navajo weavers and families who have shared their thoughts and lives with me. I thank Kit Schweitzer, my husband, and Gloria Ross, my frequent traveling partner, for encouraging my research. The Department of Anthropology at Arizona State University provided sabbatical leave during the fall 1993, and the Museum of Northern Arizona provided a quiet refuge for putting my own thoughts on paper.

32